HOW TO START A BUSINESS DURING THE PANDEMIC

Spot business opportunities during times of crisis and build a successful business from scratch.

I0116122

SUSANA PEREZ

HOW TO START A BUSINESS DURING THE PANDEMIC: Spot business opportunities during times of crisis and build a successful business from scratch.

Copyright © 2020 by Susana Perez and Creativo Publishing

ALL RIGHTS RESERVED. This book contains material protected under Federal and International Copyright Laws and Treaties. Any reprinting or unauthorized use of this material is prohibited. No part of this book may be reproduced or transmitted in any form or by any means, electronic or mechanical, including photocopying, recording, or by any information storage and retrieval system, without the express written permission of the author/publisher.

First edition 2020

Ebook ISBN- 978-1-7357071-2-9
Paperback ISBN- 978-1-7357071-3-6

Printed in the United States of America

Trademark names, logos and images may appear in this book. Instead of using a trademark symbol with every appearance of a name, logo, or image of a trademark, we use the names, logos, and images only in an editorial manner and for the benefit of the trademark owner, without intent to infringe the trademark.

The use in this publication of trade names, trademarks, service marks and similar terms, even if not identified as such, should not be taken as an expression of opinion on whether or not they are subject to proprietary rights.

Although the advice and information in this book is believed to be true and accurate at the time of publication, neither the author, nor the publisher can accept legal responsibility for any errors or omissions that may be made. The publisher makes no warranty, express or implied, about the material contained in this document.

TABLE OF CONTENTS

CHAPTER NINE

INTRODUCTION

The coronavirus pandemic has changed the world, in a way no one has seen before. It has introduced new modes of doing business, and has also rearranged our priorities. As a forward-thinking individual, you have to understand that the pandemic presents unique opportunities as well. What better way to tap into the opportunities than through starting a business of your own.

It could seem like a foolhardy thing to do at the moment. Similarly, it might appear herculean, insurmountable even. However, you have to realize first that there is nothing impossible if you put your mind to it. In any case, you have help. In this book, you will find a discussion on the reasons this is the best possible time to start and run your own business. You will also find ten best businesses you can start in this period. Finally, if you are worried about funding and how your business can survive, we have you covered. You will also find how to obtain funds and the strategies to implement to make sure your business is well ahead of others. Dig in!

CHAPTER ONE

WHY YOU SHOULD START A BUSINESS IN THE PANDEMIC

Starting a business in the thick of the pandemic might seem like a crazy idea. People are barely getting by, keeping up with the many changes that are resulting from the pandemic. Beginning a business may seem like a bad idea, with this period seeming like bad timing. However, this may not necessarily be the case. In the first place, there is precedent for businesses began at less-than-ideal moments that went on to flourish, generating millions of dollars in the future. A case in point is General Motors and IBM were both started just around the period of the Great Depression. Similarly, Facebook and Twitter were all founded following the recession of 2008. Additionally, there may be unique factors that could make this pandemic an ideal time for you to begin your business. Every crisis presents opportunities for catering to specific needs and thus creates room for new consumers and clients.

Regardless of the period, what is necessary for starting a business is an idea that solves a need. At the moment, there is a yawning, gaping need that demands to be solved. Systems of interaction and business conduct have all been changed in the wake of the pandemic. An example is how necessary social distancing has made remote work. Also, what forms entertainment and recreation have all changed, with people having to find ways to have fun within the confines of their homes. All of these changes have evolved needs that did not exist prior to the coronavirus pandemic. Asides these, there are a few other reasons to start a business during the pandemic. Find a few of them below:

1. Stronger possibility of hitting a home run

If you are able to run a successful business during this pandemic, then you can run a business anywhere and succeed. Additionally, setting up a business in these times makes you stronger when the pandemic ends. The economy is at an all-time low. Thus, if you are able to survive with the odds stacked high against you as they are at the moment, your business will be able to navigate the muddy waters of the economy.

2. Access to a lot of talented people

One fallout of the pandemic is that a lot of folks are out of jobs. The worst-hit are small businesses. Non-essential workers are being laid off to enable businesses to channel resources towards other endeavors. The same can be said of big companies and startups. They are equally laying off members of staff as a measure to stem the effects of the virus. While this is regrettable, and indeed sad, it can work to your advantage as an entrepreneur. In the first place, it means that a lot of talent is available for hire. One crucial problem businesses and startup face is lack of manpower. However, with the massive layoffs, you most certainly will have a surplus of personnel to hire and make part of your team. Additionally, these new workers will come at a cheap rate. The reason for this is simple: when the market is saturated with a particular product, its price shoots down. Simply put, because there are a lot of folks willing to work, the general rate demanded by each person will be reduced.

Asides employees, this period also gives you the opportunity to find co-founders, as well as investors. You will be sure to find people who are willing to collaborate with you on your project. Folks are available, waiting for the next idea to jump on. As for investors, it is also possible to find those in the pandemic. Generally, investors are not so keen on funding any venture, given the global state of the economy. However, some select investors do not mind pumping in money into a new venture right now. You only have to discover these investors and then pitch your ideas directly to them. Furthermore, there are grants being made available to small businesses and startups globally. Most countries have made provisions for such aids and grants, bearing in mind the devastation that the pandemic has wrought. You only have to find out if your home country has any such provisions and then apply for them. Apart from country-specific financial aids, there are aids granted by international bodies like the IMF and the World Bank. These grants are targeted mostly towards small and medium businesses begun during the pandemic. You stand a greater chance of getting these funds if your business aims to solve a problem necessitated by the pandemic. Thus, as you can see, funding and getting investors will not be a challenge if you are truly interested in beginning a business during this pandemic.

3. Businesses thrive better in crisis situations

Think of any business that is making waves at the moment. Consider them carefully. What makes them stand out in this period of the pandemic? It is most likely that they are solving a problem within this crisis. That is the secret to thriving for any business.

Beginning a business in this period will mean that you will have to grapple with a lot more challenges than the average. Additionally, you will have to find a way to thrive despite the pandemic. This would mean that you will have to have a product or service that is currently relevant. In addition, you will need to be innovative in the way you deploy the plans. All of these will help you develop the necessary skills that you need to thrive both during and after the pandemic. Truly, there may be no singular factor that makes businesses begun during the pandemic able to thrive beyond businesses started at other times. However, the fact that the business owner already knows that the tide is against them, and then works bearing this one fact in mind could make all the difference.

CHAPTER TWO

CLEANING BUSINESS

A home/office cleaning business is one of the easiest ventures to begin. It requires precious little in terms of capital –you only need to purchase the chemicals and cleaning agents you need. Furthermore, you do not need to have any sort of formal training for you to begin. Also, the business has the potentials of being very financially rewarding.

Before you start out, however, here are a few things you should know:

1. Target market

Do not just jump into the business without defining your target market. Are your proposed clientele homeowners or business people? To arrive at the answer to this, you need to take into consideration proximity to your home, convenience, as well as the people in your locality. This will, of course, mean that you have to carry out some research before beginning.

2. Budgeting

One way to run into danger is to begin your business without drawing up a budget. This is true for whatever business you want to venture into. In drawing up a budget, consider how much you will make, against how much you will send for transportation, supplies, etc.

3. Stick to a specialty

People often make the mistake of not defining what exactly their skill sets are. You will get better at your job if you focus on a single area. For instance, you could focus on carpet cleaning or just random home cleaning. After deciding on a niche, you will then have to buy the pieces of equipment and tools you need. Remember that while starting out, you may not have all the resources that you need. Hence, you might want to start small. Leave off the heavy equipment and tools for later when you can afford them.

4. Marketing

As a new entrant into the business, you have to understand that you will battle fierce opposition. The only way to close the gap and obtain a fighting chance is through aggressive marketing. First, make use of word-of-mouth marketing.

Have family and friends recommend you to others. Also, you can make use of social media. Social media is a great place to identify new clients and bond with old ones.

HOW TO THRIVE IN THE PANDEMIC

With the emergence of the coronavirus pandemic, businesses are engaging in pivotal strategies to keep them ahead. Clients are often wary of letting strangers (or non-family members) into their homes. Thus, your business may suffer as a result. However, you can anticipate and reassure your clients of your competence even during the pandemic.

For instance, you can put up information concerning the pandemic on your website. Alternatively, you can print out leaflets containing the essentials that everyone should know to keep safe in the pandemic. Let your customers know the strategies you are employing to combat the virus. If you have some new tech products or are implementing a compulsory use of masks by staff members, you should talk about this as well. Disseminating accurate information is one way to show your clients that you are truly on top of the situation. Furthermore, you can explain how your cleaning company intends to fight the virus. One popular mode of transmission for the coronavirus is through flat surfaces. If you can convince your clients that you are able to disinfect their surfaces, keeping them safe from the virus, that will surely be a plus for you. The truth is, your cleaning company could actually help protect your customers from the spread of the virus. However, they will not be aware of this. It is your responsibility to inform them. Finally, other strategies could include booking sessions in advance. You can have your cleaning periods when no one is home—this way, limiting contact with your customers or any member of their families.

CHAPTER THREE

FOOD TRUCKS

You must have seen one of those large trucks parked outside of your window, with people queuing up to purchase food from it. That is a food truck. It has become one of the fastest ways of monetizing your passion for cooking. A food truck is one idea you can explore during this pandemic. It gives you the flexibility you need to generate income while doing something that you love.

A food truck is a large vehicle with a kitchen for preparing food. The food is prepared in real-time and customers purchase in paper bags. In some cases, food trucks can be paired with delivery services. Here, customers order food by calling in or making their choice online, and the food is delivered to them by dispatch riders. Given the nature of the food truck business, there are a few things to bear in mind while starting one.

1. Conduct extensive research

Before you even buy a food truck, you should conduct

extensive surveys. The internet has made research relatively easy these days. You can find all of the information you need concerning food trucks on the internet. However, you may want to conduct on-site/physical researches. Thus, you could visit the locality where you intend the food truck to be located. Scouting the area will give you a fair idea of the number of trucks in the area. Also, you can make inquiries from existing food van owners. You can ask questions regarding what you need to know about the process.

2. Cost

Another vital consideration you should have before starting a food truck is cost. People usually start food truck businesses because they lack the means of buying or building actual brick restaurants. Thus, on a large scale, a food truck ought to be cheaper than running a full-scale restaurant business. However, it is still quite expensive.

The costs of operating a food truck are divided into one-off or recurring costs. One-off costs include the amount to purchase the food truck, website design, Point of Sale system (POS), etc. Owners often make the mistake of thinking that the major cost to pay attention to is the cost of the truck. However, there are other considerations too. At the initial stage, you will have to pay government rates and levies, including health and fire regulations. Also, you may have to hire a lawyer to make sure that you are on the right side of the law. There are other recurring costs, such as the ones for equipment rental, payment for licenses and permits, etc. Do bear in mind that the cost of starting a food truck may vary slightly, depending on your location.

3. Create a business plan.

Please note that no one will take you seriously as an entrepreneur if you do not have a business plan. It goes without saying at this point that if you are looking to start a food truck business, then you are an entrepreneur. When you reach out to investors to request for funds, when you apply for loans, grants, and other financial aids, one thing that will always be required from you is a business plan. An excellent business plan has the following sections: executive summary, company description, market analysis, funding request, financial projections, etc.

A key aspect of your business plan is your budget. A budget forms part of your business plan and is a crucial part in determining the success of your food truck business. First, you need to outline all of the costs, as enumerated above. Then write out the means of sourcing for funds for all of the items you listed. The budget simply gives you a bird's eye view of all you gathered during your research process. Thus, you won't be doing anything new at this point.

4. Craft a marketing plan

You are headed for disaster if you rush into the food truck business without a marketing strategy. This is because your marketing strategy informs how you make sales. Who do you sell to? At what rate, and at what location? Etc. A solid marketing strategy involves several tactics. You can make use of the traditional marketing strategies such as direct mail messaging and media adverts. You can also decide to go for digital marketing strategies. In doing this, you incorporate tactics related to Search Engine Optimization (SEO), Facebook ads, and even email marketing. You should make sure that your plan is flexible so that you could change or incorporate more features at any point where things don't seem to be working fine.

Whatever you do, pay keen attention to social media

marketing. This is because it is the rave at the moment. You can scarcely find any serious business without a stable social media online presence. As a food truck owner, you should key into this. On social media, share everything about your business. Have customers drop reviews and recommendations on your pages. It will help you get you followers. Also, organize contests, giveaways, and other social media marketing ideas to get people interested in your business.

OPERATING A FOOD TRUCK DURING THE PANDEMIC

You have to understand that some food truck strategies have to be tweaked to fit into the current situation. With the coronavirus pandemic and stipulations regarding social distancing, there may be concerns regarding the safety of food truck businesses - both from the government and private citizens. These concerns may relate to health, adhering to regulations, etc. Thus, as a food truck owner, you have to be ingenious in your plans and strategies. For instance, instead of waiting for customers to line up outside your truck, you can drive to meet them. The focus on social distancing has made it that people are not so keen on stepping outside of their homes. Additionally, they are more likely to cook food themselves instead of ordering out. Again, this could mean that you have to change your clientele. You can look for neighborhoods where you hadn't been to before. You can decide to check out hospitals and residential neighborhoods. This move could score you a few new customers. You can also decide to park your truck along highways and rest trucks. Most restaurants are not open to full capacity. They are thus unable to assimilate all of the customers that stop by during their journeys. But with your truck at rest stops and along highways, you can intercept and take advantage of this group. Do not worry about obtaining permits and the likes. The Federal Highway Administration grants states the liberty to issue highway permits. When you obtain one of those, you will be good to go!

You can also decide to have a deal with essential business owners. Businesses in this category include those that are mandated to remain open because of the nature of the products/services they provide. Here you find businesses that sell health supplies, etc. You can come to an agreement with these business owners, and they'll let you park your truck in front of theirs. In this way, you will be taking advantage of the regular supply of clientele that these businesses have.

CHAPTER FOUR

ONLINE GAMING

Gaming is the rave of the moment. This is applicable to both gamers themselves and gaming business operators. You only need look at the number of online gaming casinos and consider how much they rake in each year to understand how big the industry is. However, this does not mean that challenges are absent. Like any true business endeavor, there are challenges that come with operating a gaming business. You have to strike the perfect balance between profitability and customer satisfaction. Hence, you need to ensure that the gaming business you start make you the profit that you seek while attracting interested gamers to your place. Additionally, you have to have a good understanding of marketing, working to ensure that the right number of gamers are aware of your business and how it could potentially benefit them.

Below, you will find a few steps and tips on how to run a successful gaming business.

1. Learn all you can about the process

You must start out by gathering as much information as you

can about the gaming business and how it works. You have to understand that the fact that you are an avid gamer yourself is hardly enough. Sure, it could help you understand consumer behavior and thus influence some choices you make in that area. However, on the whole, this knowledge may not be entirely useful in other areas, hence the need to study. Find out as much as you can about the gaming business, what it entails, and how you could be successful at it. You have to bear in mind that this is not something that can be achieved in a short period. You have to dedicate some to the venture. Therefore, you have to map out a specific period to carry out intensive learning by reading articles, compiling news headlines, carrying out target research, etc.

2. Begin with a business plan

After carrying out your extensive research, the next thing to do is to write a business plan. A business plan is the perfect way to put all you have learned into black and white. The business plan will give a concise view of what you intend to achieve over a specific period. While writing your business plan, do make sure that you adhere to best practices. You need to include items such as what kind of games you intend to host, location: physical or virtual, etc. You also have to make sure you have figured out information relating to costs before starting the business plan. Costs and considerations that come with it should have been figured out at the learning stage. Thus, in your business plan, you should include your projected earnings and expenditure, including the cost of leases or rental space, the cost of appropriate licenses, and payment of a legal officer. Also, it is important that you define clearly what kind of business you want to run. There are some options for you to explore. For instance, you could decide to go with a sole proprietorship or a partnership. Finally, also include your target market. Make sure that you are specific and clear about the numbers. Of course, you may have to employ an expert to help you figure out this part. Whatever you do, make sure that you get the numbers correctly calculated.

3. Sort out the legalities

There are a couple of legal issues you have to sort out if your gaming business is going to get off right. This is because for most gaming and gambling casinos, being on the wrong side of the law is the norm. You should make sure that you do not run your gaming business that way. Getting the law on your side is always a solid plan that you cannot get wrong with. Thus, at this point, you should be thinking of licenses, jurisdiction, and the applications you have to make to make sure you do not run into challenges in that aspect.

You should be careful when deciding on the jurisdiction you want to set up shop in. Different countries have their separate requirements, as well as the sort of incentives they make available for businesses. Make sure you do the due diligence and carry out sufficient research before settling for any jurisdiction. Make sure you carefully weigh the pros and cons of each jurisdiction. Also, if you intend to have your gaming sites to be used by individuals across several countries, you also have to figure out the jurisdictional issues related to that. For instance, you may have to grapple with different rules for the different countries, making sure you do not run afoul of the law at any point.

After sorting out the issues relating to jurisdiction, you need to figure out the legal form of your business. You might be required to decide on the form of business you want to run. Generally, you can register your business either as a private or public entity. There are risks and perks associated with each form. Additionally, you have to factor in the funds you have, whether you have partners, the jurisdiction you are operating in, etc., before then making a decision. Each country has requirements it demands from those seeking to register their businesses. Also, you may want to employ the services of a lawyer. This might cost a little more than the average, but it helps make sure that you avoid mistakes in the future.

4. Deciding on the software

The last (or one of the last things) you have to consider is the software for your gaming business. Depending on the peculiarities of your business, you will need your customers to interact with you through some means. Additionally, they will have to play the game on a platform. That platform will be your software. Luckily for you, there are quite a number of providers able and willing to provide you with the software that you can host your business with. A few things you have to check off before settling for any include making sure that the software is popular and offers a simple user interface. Also, any such software should come with features that include a player management system, payment system management interface, reporting engine, encryption software, retention email system, tech support system, etc. Software that ticks off all of the boxes mentioned might be a bit pricey. However, this is an investment you should be willing to make. This is because, in the long run, you will be better off for making a choice to pay this huge one-off price.

SURVIVING THE CORONAVIRUS PANDEMIC

The good news with this business idea is that you are hardly impacted by the pandemic and the social distancing requirements that come with it. In the first place, gamers are widely known to be recluses. They spend their days focused on their gaming device without having to step out. Hence, you can rest assured that your client base will not be impacted on account of the pandemic. Similarly, your business model will not be affected by the pandemic, too. You can run your gaming business totally online without having to come in contact with your customers. Your customers also will not have to be mindful of coming in contact with one another. A gaming business is perhaps the ideal business for staying ahead of government regulations during the coronavirus pandemic.

CHAPTER FIVE

DOG BREEDING BUSINESS

If you are a dog-lover, you may want to indulge your love for pets by starting a dog breeding business. Of course, while you are enthusiastic and pumped up about the process of beginning the dog breeding business, you may lose sight of the enormous amount of work required. For your dog breeding business to be successful, you will need to invest an enormous amount of time and commitment into making it work. It also requires time. This is because you will have to be patient to wait for the dog to go through the different periods of gestation and then birth healthy puppies for you to sell. More so, dog breeds come with their own unique needs. Whether you want to start breeding Rottweilers, Dobermans, or Pit Bulls, you have to learn about that specific breed before commencing. Not to worry, in this guide, you will find the basic things you have to know before beginning a dog breeding business.

Tips for Running a Successful Dog Breeding Business in the Pandemic

1. Decide on a dog breed

You have to decide on the breed of dog you want to start grooming. As pointed out above, the care and attention you will give to your dogs will depend on their breed. Similarly, your breed of choice will depend on the prominent roles the dogs are used for. There are dogs for the elderly, patrol dogs, security dogs, dogs for the visually impaired, etc.

Please bear in mind that to run a breeding business, you need both male and female dogs. If this is too expensive, you can decide to buy online female dogs and then have them mate with another breeder's male dog. This is a regular practice in the industry. Usually, the owner of the male dog requires a small fee. However, that could be easily negotiated. Also, if you make this a regular practice with the dog owner, you could get discounts while at it.

2. Fix issues relating to location

The next important issue to sort out is the facility that will house your dogs. The facility should be appropriate. This means that you have to pay specific attention to hygiene requirements, ventilation, space, etc. The quality of your facilities is very important, especially with regard to insurance. Furthermore, in the unlikely event that a tragedy occurs, the amount of compensation you will be entitled to will depend on the quality of your facilities.

3. Hire the right people/Tools that you need

Whether you will hire employees to work with you on your business will depend on your scale. If you intend to run a small dog-breeding enterprise, you may not need to get any external help involved. At most, you may have to get one other person to get involved with you. Additionally, the amount of time you want to dedicate to the business will also affect whether you hire help or not. For instance, if you intend to have the business on a part-time basis, then you will most likely need to get some support staff. It is advisable that since you are beginning the business from scratch, you start small. This will be best in order to reduce the possibilities of running into challenges, and also for managing such challenges when they occur.

In the same vein, you need certain tools/equipment to ensure that your business is off to a good start. The items you need include a kennel, food supplements, food supplies, drugs, etc.

4. Expect Challenges

Just like every other business, dog breeding comes with its own set of unique challenges you have to tackle. One challenge is the fact that you may not have a stable monthly income breeding dogs. This is because you cannot breed dogs every month. Thus, you have to look for another source of income. Also, advertising could present an obstacle. The amount you make within each period is dependent on the number of pups you sell. However, sales may not come as frequently as you wish/like. This places the extra burden of looking for buyers on you. Finally, dog breeding can be quite expensive. You have to factor in the cost of getting the pups, the cost of running the veterinary tests you need to carry out, including genetic tests, too. In all, it could well be an expensive venture. You have to make sure that you have thoroughly 'counted the costs' before beginning.

CHAPTER SIX

DOG GROOMING

Dog grooming is similar to dog breeding in that one should only venture into it for the love of dogs. Dog grooming essentially refers to all that is concerned with taking care of your dog. This does not replace the need for a vet. In fact, the two roles are distinct.

In the animal service industry, pet grooming, particularly dog grooming, is booming. According to the American Pet Products Association, more than 63 million American homes have dogs. This gives you an endless supply of clients for your grooming business. What are the essentials that you need to be aware of for your breeding business yo take off smoothly? A few of them are discussed below.

1. Learn all you can about the process.

Dog grooming is no walk in the park, contrary to what you must have heard. For you to be successful, you have to develop some expertise in the area. You can acquire this knowledge either by taking a professional course and getting certificated, or you can learn from someone established in the business.

2. Consider the nature of the Business

Next, you have to figure out the format this business will take. There are a couple of options to consider. You can either decide to run a sole proprietorship, a partnership or a limited liability company. For each option, there are benefits and drawbacks. For instance, governments usually give tax incentives to businesses to help them start up smoothly. In any case, to avoid any confusion, you might want to refer to an attorney to walk you through the process.

3. Equipment and Tools

Equipment and tools will take up a substantial part of your budget while starting up. The grooming business is heavily dependent on the number of tools you have available. The more you have, the easier it is. Items you need include clippers, dog shampoo, ear cleaning products, bandanas, etc.

4. Settle on a marketing plan

This should be the last port of call when starting a dog grooming business. Do make sure that you have a marketing strategy already mapped out. Always keep the competition in view. You can decide to leverage social media, creating a business page solely dedicated to your business. You can also liaise with veterinary doctors, dog walkers, etc. They could send you referrals, and you do the same for them, too.

RUNNING A DOG GROOMING BUSINESS DURING THE PANDEMIC

Your business may be impacted by the pandemic and the restrictions imposed by countries. In the first place, dog grooming is not an essential service - although there have been arguments in several quarters that it actually is, and should be accorded that privilege. Thus, dog grooming businesses have not been granted the exception of being open regardless of the pandemic. In some countries, the social distancing rules have been lifted, and businesses are free to open. However, there are strict rules regarding what times the businesses are to open and their modes of operation. Thus, you have to be strict with your adherence to the rules stipulated in your jurisdiction. Additionally, you can take some precautionary measures. For instance, you can decide to have home visits instead of having your clients bring their dogs over to your place of work. Furthermore, you can also have clients call in and book appointments before showing up. This will help you regulate the rate at which people are physically present at your location. Finally, you should make sanitation items available. Facilities for washing of hands, gloves, and face masks should also be available where necessary.

CHAPTER SEVEN

BODY CARE PRODUCTS (SKIN AND HAIR CARE)

Most people generally care about their skin and hair. However, proper skin care requires dedication and time. Time, the pandemic has given us time in abundance. Dedication, one has to build personally. Now people can adequately care for their skin and hair. But people need skin and hair care products. There are three broad fields you can start this business in. they are:

- Selling body care products
- Selling information on body care products
- Starting a body care products line

Of the three of them, the most difficult to start is the product line. Starting a line will require the actors of production and capital, which you may not have. The easiest to start are the first two. You can start a blog on different body care products and their suitability for different classes of people. You can also restrict your information dissemination to social media platforms. Established and upcoming body care product lines may now have to pay you to put out information about their products. You can also package body products information and sell these online. This aspect of the business will usually require little or no capital at all.

You can also sell body care products. This can be done without the body care products information business. However, it will be better to combine both. This is because your clientele in the information business will find it easy to buy any products you sell. You may need to partner with products lines to get their products in bulk. The partnership will also guarantee cheaper prices. And, if you don't fully have the start-up capital, you can rely on credit financing until your business grows.

CHAPTER EIGHT

TUTORING

With the pandemic, academic activities were disrupted in many institutions, with many resorting to online learning. But, can everyone learn properly online? The pandemic has also given everyone the time to learn not just out of necessity, but also because of an interest in the subject matter. People who have specific learning interests can capitalize on the excess time to learn what they truly desire. Here are some tutoring opportunities:

1. Teach a foreign language

If you are proficient in a foreign language, you could start teaching it. Your clients could include a young professional who requires proficiency in a foreign language to increase his job prospects, or even a young student applying to a foreign school. This business could be virtual or physical, or both.

2. Teach special needs kids

Time again, the pandemic has given everyone the time to learn something they've truly desired to learn, such as a foreign language or a musical instrument.

3. Teach pre-schoolers:

A lot of parents are stuck at home with their pre-school kids. Some of these kids are seriously hampering their parent's productivity. You could start teaching such kids from the comfort of your home. Here, you don't need to go too far for your target market. Pre-schoolers are everywhere, even in your own neighborhood. You also don't require any special academic qualifications to teach pre-schoolers. All you need is patience in abundance.

4. Help students catch up

Some students also require a higher level of supervision, which cannot be provided virtually. You can teach such students, providing very direct supervision and monitoring for them. Such students are not widely distributed. Therefore, you may need to engage some form of target marketing to get your desired clients.

The good thing about tutoring as a job is that no one child can take up all or most of your time. This isn't babysitting. Thus, you can teach multiple kids and even combine teaching the different classes of students mentioned above.

CHAPTER NINE

FITNESS AND HEALTH

With minimal work and physical activity, many people will develop bad eating habits. And bad eating habits will result in poor health and low physical fitness. Here comes in the entrepreneur – to help people back to the path of physical fitness and good health. The wellness industry is one of the fastest-growing in the world.

Fitness refers to a state of physical and mental soundness with good health. Conventionally, fitness is frequently related to physical fitness. Health is wider. Health is the state of being free from illness or injury - a state of complete well being. For a health business, you could start a blog on mental health awareness. There are many popular sections of fitness and health. They include:

- Food and Nutrition
- Healthy Eating and Dieting
- Gym Facilities and Exercising

1. **Fitness and Health Retreats:**
You can also organize fitness and health retreats. Here you

can organize people for intensive retreats. In these retreats, all forms of fitness and health will be taught and practiced.

2. One-Stop Shop Wellness Centers:

You can also start a one-stop-shop for all fitness and health needs. From exercise equipment to food supplements; even health information can be packaged and sold there.

3. Personal Training:

You can work as a personal trainer for people. People interested in weight loss or bodybuilding may require personal trainers.

4. Fitness and Health Blogging and Vlogging

You could start a fitness and health blog. Or you could go further. You can also sell fitness courses and tutorials. Also, podcasts are becoming a thing. So, a fitness podcast will not be a bad idea.

5. Personal Chefs:

You can also specialize as a personal chef. It is also an added bonus if you have an added knowledge on nutrition. You can tailor your client's food to their specific food needs.

6. Health Coach

You could also be a health coach. A health coach will generally help people lead all-round healthier lives. This will include helping people

7. Mental Health Awareness

The world is increasingly taking mental health seriously. And while you may not be qualified to act as a therapist, there are still opportunities in creating awareness. You could start out disseminating information on mental health. You could focus on basic issues such as the signs of mental illness, types of mental illness, causes and effects, etc. information on these basics can be readily sourced on the internet and made available to your audience. You could also take courses on this online. Online certifications boost your credibility and increase your knowledge bank.

8. Brand Management

Even if you don't want to go through the process of building your own brand, there is still a job for you. You could also work on building fitness brands online. There are a lot of fitness brands and personalities online. Fitness brands will also require blog posts and pictures or someone to generally manage their websites. Some fitness personalities will also need someone to properly manage their brand for them. These are jobs that can be done remotely on social media without physical contact.

9. Photography

There is also an opportunity in the fitness industry for photographers and video editors. Fitness personalities obviously need someone to take pictures and videos of their bodies and workout sessions. This they cannot do for themselves. So, if you have any photography skills, this could be the job for you.

There are many other business opportunities in the fitness and health sector. You could work as a yoga instructor, a massage therapist, dancing studios: dancing is becoming a popular form of exercise and a means to keep fit.

CHAPTER TEN

INVESTMENT MANAGEMENT

The pandemic has brought about a loss of jobs for a lot of people. There's a chance that as you are reading this you know someone who has lost a job because of the pandemic. Or you could even be that someone. Any person who has spare cash would love to learn about how such cash can be put to good use with minimal engagement on the part of the funder. Here lies the employment opportunity for you. While searching for a new job, a recently laid-off person can start out as an investment manager.

Investment management is the professional asset management of various securities and other assets in order to meet specific investment goals for the investor. Assets you could manage include shares, bonds, and other securities. You can also manage real estate. Investors for you could be people with spare cash lying around. You can also manage major assets.

Investment management for you can take two spheres shapes. You can go into pure asset management. Here you will manage actual assets for people. You could also choose to only restrict yourself to giving information on asset management and investment.

Here are some tips on how to become an investment manager during this lockdown:

1. Take some courses on investment management

There are many courses on investment management on online learning platforms such as Coursera. This is especially necessary if you have no prior knowledge of investment management. You may also have prior knowledge of the field but no official certifications. Online certifications from reputable universities will help build your portfolio and credibility.

A good thing is that on most online learning platforms, you can fast track your learning. The idea is that you don't have the time to wait for the entire duration of the course. You can also run multiple courses and have multiple certifications.

2. Get Acquainted with Online Investment Management Websites

Online investment management websites will feature articles on investment management written by professionals. Getting acquainted with these websites serves two functions. It serves as a source of continuing education on investment management. And it also informs you of new investment opportunities.

3. Establish an online portfolio as an investment manager

It is stating the obvious to say that every business should have an online presence. Starting as an investment manager, you need to create a portfolio online. This would include social media platforms such as Facebook and Twitter. Also utilize the professional social media platform LinkedIn. Post information on investment management on these platforms frequently. This will help you get new clients.

You can start out managing the investments of your family and friends. Then have them endorse you online for a job. Such endorsements will get you more jobs in their circle.

4. Register

If you try out this business and decide you want to go big-time, you must do some registrations. You should register your company with the state. After this, you should register with the Securities and Exchange Commission (SEC). Investment management companies are required to register with the SEC.

CHAPTER ELEVEN

SELF-PUBLISHING ON AMAZON

Self-publishing a book is hard. It is hard to get them into local and international libraries worldwide. It is harder for self-published works. Amazon provides an opportunity for writers to independently publish their works on their platform. Kindle Direct Publishing is Amazon's publishing unit, which was launched in November 2007. It started out with only an e-publishing option. In 2016, the paperback option was added. Now, anyone can publish either paperbacks or eBooks on Amazon; or both.

The obvious advantage is that you have access to the already existing millions of readers on Amazon. Amazon puts your book at the very place people are looking for books. By publishing on Amazon, you escape the high costs of publishing.

Why should you self publish on Amazon? Amazon highlights five advantages of self-publishing with them. They are:

1. Getting to the market fast: From the comfort of your bedroom, you can publish your book and have it on Kindle stores worldwide. All this in about 24-48 hours. This dispenses with the drudgery of physically sending your books to hardcopy stores that have limited reaches.

2. You make more money: Amazon also guarantees 70% royalty on sales to their customers in the US and many more countries. KDP Select on Amazon also promises higher returns. Here you can earn more money through Kindle Unlimited and Kindle Owner's Lending Library.

3. Keep Control: Publishing on Amazon also retain control of your rights. You can also fix the prices of your books as you see fit. And if you want to make any changes to your books, you can do so just as easily as you published the book.

4. Publish in Digital and Print: with Amazon, you have the option of publishing both hard and soft copies of your book. The world is generally divided along the lines of those who love to read hard copy books and

those who prefer softcopies. By publishing on Amazon, you are able to reach both audiences.

How do you go about publishing on Amazon? Below are the steps to take to self-publish on Amazon:

1. Set Up your account

The first thing you must do is set up an account on Amazon KDP. You can also link the account with your current Amazon account. After creating your account, you will need to fill in your author information.

2. Format your book

You will need to convert your eBook for publication. Amazon has a program for this – Amazon Kindle Create.

3. Your Book Cover

Your book obviously needs a book cover. Here, you have some options. Cover Creator is a tool on Amazon KDP with which you can create your book cover. You can make it by yourself and upload. You can also employ someone to design your own book cover.

At the upload stage, you will need to fill in the book details (author, title, subtitle, book description). You will also need to choose the Book category. Next, you will upload the book and preview it. This is to make sure it looks good. After this stage is the pricing stage where you can choose where you want your book to be published and select your royalty plan. Once all this is done, you can submit your book for review, after which you can begin selling. Congratulations! You are now a published author.

CHAPTER TWELVE

WAYS TO GENERATE FUNDS FOR BUSINESS

A major issue for those intending to start businesses is how to raise their start-up capital. Having a good idea is great; but only capital can translate ideas to reality. There are a lot of ways one can generate funds for their business. Some are basic and traditional, while some are unconventional. Below are some ways you can generate funds to start your business:

SELF FUNDING

As long as your business is not in a sector that requires heavy start-up capital, it is very possible to self-fund it. This is also called bootstrapping. Self-funding can be divided into two categories. They are:

Personal savings; and

Sale of personal assets.

PERSONAL SAVINGS

The primary means of self-funding a business is through

personal savings. If you have plans to start a business, it is only advisable that you begin saving towards the business.

There are some advantages to the self-funding option. For example, personal savings is the only source of funds generation over which the potential business owner has absolute control. Every other source of generating funds can prove unreliable or even fail. Personal funds also come with minimal risks. If such funds are invested in the business and lost, you will not be under any pressure to repay such money. Personal savings also show the business person's level of commitment to the business plan. And if you have to source for extra funding, such commitment may further convince a potential investor.

PERSONAL ASSETS SALE

Every individual old enough to start a business will most likely have personal have assets that can be sold to fund the startup. This funding option depends on two factors. The required start-up capital, and how buoyant you are. Where the startup requires relatively small capital, you can sell small assets such as electronic gadgets. But where higher capital is needed, houses and lands may need to be sold. This is only if you have such assets.

RAISING CAPITAL FROM FAMILY AND FRIENDS

You can also raise capital from your friends and family. According to the Global Entrepreneurship Monitor, 5% of US adults have invested in a company started by someone they know. Family and friends are usually the easiest to be convinced about a business idea. They already have first-hand experience and information as to your credibility and capacity. Therefore, they usually require less convincing than venture capitalists and other types of investors. Such belief and trust usually also translates into funding for the business. Basically, they are investing in you as much as they are investing in your business.

A rich family member or friend may be sufficient to offset the initial capital requirements of the business. Conversely, multiple family members and/or friends could each contribute little amounts to pool large resources. One advantage of this form of lending over other forms of lending is that such funds usually come as low or non-interest loans. Close friends or family members are most likely to lend you money without interest. Thus, you will have to repay only the initial loan. Some of such funds may even be gifts, with no expectation of repayment.

CROWD FUNDING

Crowdfunding is an upgrade of the family and friends' option. There are multiple successful crowdfunding stories. From crowdfunding for education to crowdfunding health needs. People have even crowdfunded their favorite celebrity or politician. So, it shouldn't be hard to successfully crowdfund your business venture. For example, farmers in Nigeria, Africa are heavily utilizing crowdfunding for agribusiness. Crowdfunding has a distinct feature. It can also help you gauge public opinion on your business plan/idea. You may also find your target market during this process.

Here are some tips to carry out a successful crowdfunding campaign:

Draft a good business plan that is easily relatable.

Use a reliable crowdfunding platform that demands accountability.

Get your close friends and associates to start donating. People are more likely to donate when they see that others are already donating.

Carefully select your target audience.

If you can get respected people in your area or field to endorse your campaign, do so. Such endorsements engender trust for you in the funders. Trust equals more funds.

BANK LOANS

Surely, technological advancements have given us some unconventional fundraising means. However, traditional fundraising schemes such as bank loans are still practical and efficient. People usually resort to bank loans where the required start-up capital is high. The obvious allure of bank loans is the fact that banks have unlimited resources. So, you can get all the funds you need from one bank. A major downside, however, is the usual requirement for collateral. A start-up is most unlikely to have the facilities for adequate collateral. Hence, start ups tend to shy away from bank loans. Another downside is the high-interest rates which may be unfavorable for businesses which haven't made any initial profits.

Where one chooses bank loans as a source of funding, the following will usually be considered by the banks before giving you the loan:

You have been in business for a while – two years and more.

Your business has strong annual revenues – actual or projected.

You have a good credit rating. Banks will not lend to people who have a history of defaulting on loans.

CREDIT FINANCING

Some businesses can be financed through credit financing or vendor financing. If your ability to pay for goods depends on your ability to sell the goods or convert them to finished products, then vendor financing is a good option for you. Vendor financing may also become necessary if you receive an unusually high demand.

Credit financing involves receiving goods on credit from a vendor with an undertaking to pay their cost at a later date. Many vendors already have such payment arrangement. You need not be the initiator. Many vendors require payment on invoices within 30 days before activating any penalties. It is also possible to negotiate a longer payment period. This is necessary if the disposal cycle for the goods is longer than what the vendor offers. However, not all vendors will accept this.

Vendor financing requires two main qualities:

Credibility and honesty of the creditor: All forms of credit borrowing require that the debtor must be trustworthy. Just like in bank loans, where a customer has a history of defaulting on credits, no vendor will finance him. Therefore, you must endeavor to be honest in all dealings. This is because you never know when you might require a credit facility.

Relationships are also important. Vendors will are more likely to finance customers with whom they already have existing relationships. Relationships beget trust. And trust is required for any credit arrangement.

ANGEL INVESTORS

Some types of businesses, such as tech startups will require more capital than any of the above funding options can provide. Angel investors are usually established business professionals with lots of cash who are looking to invest in promising companies.

Angel investors usually work in groups. They screen proposals together before deciding to invest. There's a case to be made for angel investors. As business professionals, they can offer business insights and wisdom to fund seekers. Even if you don't get the funds, specific insights into your business are added advantages. Angel investors have helped some popular companies such as Google, Yahoo and Alibaba. However, they usually require some form equity ownership in the business.

The connections of these angel investors can be easily gotten from fellow entrepreneurs. Angel investors also have associations or websites such as the Angel Capital Association and AngelList. Beyond direct funding of businesses, angel investors also host competitions and events. An aim of such events is to afford entrepreneurs further contacts.

VENTURE CAPITALISTS

Need larger funds? A million dollars and above? You could consider venture capitalists. Venture capitalists typically have more funds than angel investors. Venture capital investment is more appropriate for businesses that have started operations and are already generating revenue. A downside is that VCs usually want to recover their investment quickly. They usually give a three to five-year window of repayment. So, if you aren't sure that you can repay within such a period, it will be unwise to approach VCs.

CONTESTS

Practically every field of endeavor has contests and competitions where the winner receives some prize money. These contests are both local and international. Here entrepreneurs are required to pitch their ideas or submit a business plan. Winning such competitions also brings free media publicity as such competitions are highly publicized. Winning requires that your pitch or business plan be outstanding. This is because the wide publicity attracts many contestants and increases the competition.

There are other forms of funds generation. They include government programs that offer startup capital and product pre-sale or pre-order. The advantages and disadvantages of the above funding options have been highlighted to help you choose which funding option is best suited for your business. Multiple funds generating options may also be combined for better results.

CHAPTER THIRTEEN

STRATEGIES FOR MAKING YOUR BUSINESS THRIVE DURING THE PANDEMIC

There are some basic strategies for growing a business. However, the strategies for growing a thriving business during this pandemic are definitely going to be different from what was required when life was normal. Creativity and uniqueness are the most required strategies to build your business during this pandemic. For example, handing out of fliers is totally off this list of strategies.

1. Digitalization and Social Media Marketing

It'll be stating the obvious to say that, in 2020, every business should have an online presence. This fact became much more glaring during this pandemic. The main strategies for getting your business to thrive during this lockdown are definitely via online media. I mean, everyone is at home doing a little more than nothing, so we all have time for social media. Statistics also show that there has been an increased online presence during this lockdown. So, you must consider and use social media marketing. Social media marketing is cheap. It may well be the cheapest form of advertising available. No billboards or TV adverts. I mean, who watches TV these days and isn't active on social media? TV audiences are just as high as social media audiences.

For businesses with many staff, implement a remote work policy. Workers need not shuttle to work and back for work they can do remotely. You save them money and increase their efficiency at the same time.

Below are some guidelines for effective social media marketing:

- On social media, start or join conversations.

- Post about your product frequently.

- You should post with trending hashtags of the day.

- You can also include product's education. You can do this for your specific products and the field in general.

- You can also do occasional giveaways. Social media has welcomed the idea of giveaways – freebies. However, yours is a business. So, you must give away money responsibly. Not frequently and not exorbitant amounts.

- Build virtual relationships. Connect with social media influencers. If possible, get them to use your products and recommend them publicly.

- Maintain your online presence. Be consistently online. You may need to hire someone who has this as a specific job. Reply request and questions from customers promptly.

- Don't get involved in controversial social media debates. This may cause you to lose customers.

2. **Narrow your advertising to your target audience**

Online advertising strategy will require some tact. This is because online advertising isn't necessarily about reaching a large audience as it is about reaching the right audience. An audience of one million who aren't your target market are useless to you. So you must narrow down your advertising to your target audience.

For tutoring above, your target audience would obviously include high schoolers and their parents. It would be silly to advertise in a group or on a page for Teachers Unions. For skin and hair care, it would be wiser to intentionally target female audiences more than their male counterparts. The reason is clear. Society is structured such that females care more about their skin than the males do.

3. Honest Communication with Customers

The pandemic has heavily affected many businesses, adversely for most. Naturally, this has resulted in a reduction of customer's confidence in businesses. However, this can be helped, such that businesses don't lose a lot of clients. In this pandemic, honesty is the best policy for your business. Businesses need to honestly communicate with consumers on how adversely they were affected by the pandemic. This then ought to be followed by assurances and steps the business is taking to mitigate and cushion any losses to customers. This will go a long way to strengthen the trust between the business and the customers. Trust here, will translate into a longer-lasting relationship.

Reassuring your customers that everything will be fine is necessary. You must show that you are concerned about your business relationship. Honest communication can be achieved through the following means:

It could be argued that such honesty on the true state of your business may work against the business. However, this isn't true. Everyone is already well acquainted with information that this pandemic has adversely affected businesses. Therefore, withholding such information is merely hiding the obvious. Conversely, such honesty could actually endear you to your customers. No one is repulsed by honesty. Everyone appreciates honesty in dealings; especially where money is involved. Therefore, any expression of honesty within this period will strengthen business relationships rather than end them.

4. **Be sensitive with your prices**

The pandemic has affected the purchasing power of many people. Therefore, this new dynamic must be considered by a business person in price-fixing. You need to be reasonable in your price-fixing. Now is not the time to try to make astronomical profits. There will be a lot of time after this pandemic to make high profits. This period is for maintaining your customer's relationships. After this pandemic, all those relationships can be leveraged for better profits.

5. Use Customer Advertising or Referrals

Since the pandemic has reduced business cash flow, your business may not have a lot of money to spend on big adverts. But you can't stop advertising altogether. You must find a cheaper means of advertising. One of such cheaper advertising forms is customer advertising or customer referrals. Here, you get satisfied customers to advertise your business either by word of mouth or on social media. They can also use any other form of advertising they choose. Any other customer who confirms that they were referred by an existing customer guarantees a referral bonus for the original customer who made the referral. The referral bonus could be anything. For a discount offer to a free gift or even a free product or free session of the service you are providing. This advert form helps strengthen the business-customer relationship. It also ensures that the business relationship is built on trust and service quality. Nothing beats advertising or recommendations from an obviously satisfied customer.

6. Donate to Covid-19 Relief Programs

This will give your business a human face. It will reassure your customers and the world at large that you are interested in their welfare and not just profits. Also, covid-19 donations are announced publicly for accountability. This is free media publicity. You should, however, donate reasonably. This is in order not to create a false impression of wealth.

7. **Consider cutting out the middlemen**

Middlemen are the ones who get your products to the final consumers. You sell at lower prices to them so that they can make their own profits. So, you need to think of how to claim those profits for yourself. Consider sending your goods directly to your customers. The advantage is clear. By eliminating the middleman, the personal profit they make becomes yours.

8. **Encourage your team**

Finally, your staff members are also going through hard times. Encourage them. Don't be hard on them. Don't make unrealistic demands of them. The goal is to get them to remain effective.

CONCLUSION

If you have gotten to this point, then you have all you need to run a successful business in this pandemic. From the list above, you can select any idea that catches your fancy. Please consider your expertise and prior knowledge before deciding on any. What this means is that if, for instance, you have a strong passion for dog breeding, then you should probably do that. It might not go as smoothly as envisioned, especially if this is your first business. However, if you keep at it, you will surely succeed.

ABOUT THE AUTHOR

Susana Pérez, owner and founder of "CREATIVO PUBLISHING".

She started her first company in 1998; a printing service serving small and medium-sized companies in Montevideo Uruguay. Susana is an enthusiastic entrepreneur who has worked in the areas of advertising, customer service, sales, graphic design, cleaning, and food industries.

Her residential cleaning company; The Queen of Chores received a 5-star recognition in her local community.

Susana was born in Montevideo, Uruguay. She was raised by a single mother with 5 children. Her mother gave her best to raise her children. She worked most of her life offering cleaning services, although she also ran her own grocery stores for a few years.

Susana never dreamed of having her own business or writing a book.

She is the only person in her family to have immigrated to the USA where she decided to pursue the American dream. Nothing was easy. She made plenty of mistakes and has started over more than once. Being the only person in her family to learn another language she faced many obstacles with immigration, being a single mother, and adjusting to a new culture and way of life.

She survived a traffic accident that left her in a coma for 10 days, a deportation order, pregnancy on her own, divorce, eviction, and being the sole provider and caretaker of her children.

As a single mother, she decided to put her family first and made every decision with them in mind. After the eviction, she spent time in a home for evicted families with her children. However, she knew she had the skills and resources that would get her through. And with her positive attitude and resilience, she faced every challenge knowing there was something better on the other side.

Today, Creativo Publishing is growing and has big plans for the future.

Susana finds a balance between spending time with her family, her dogs Shilo and Sophie, friends who are often enterprising like her, reading, writing, listening to music, dancing Salsa and Bachata or getting lost in the trails of Utah's Rocky Mountains where she finds peace and quiet.

Find Susana on: Facebook:

www.facebook.com/susana.perez.us

Website: www.susanaperez.us

www.ingramcontent.com/pod-product-compliance
Lightning Source LLC
Chambersburg PA
CBHW060518280326
41933CB00014B/3011

* 9 7 8 1 7 3 5 7 0 7 1 3 6 *